Harry Potter for kids

This Book belongs to:

_____

1
Start the head

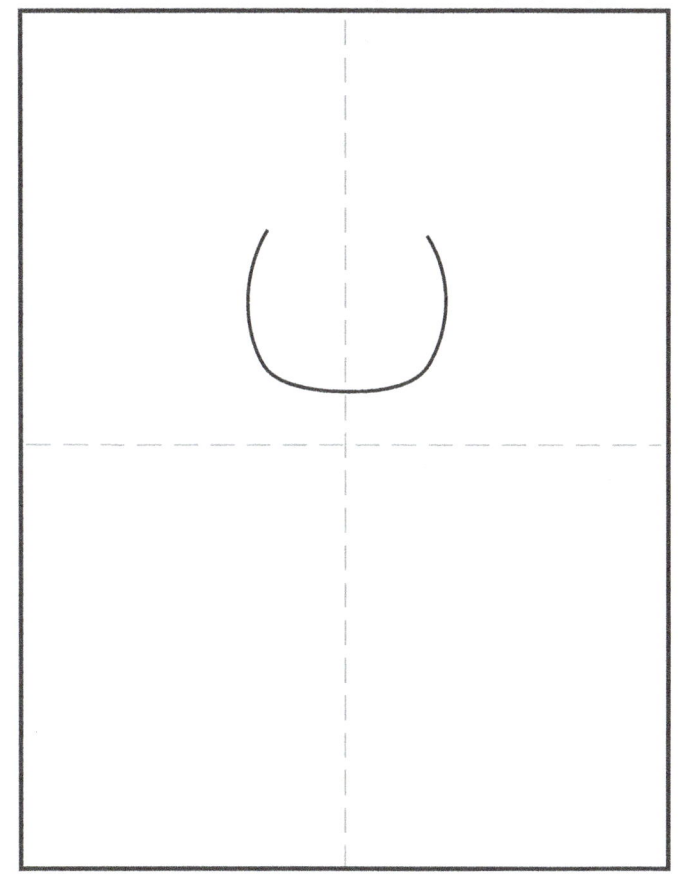

2
Add bangs on top, and ears

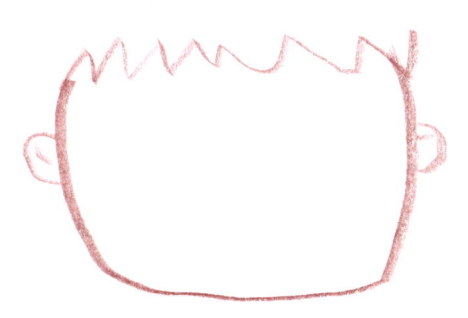

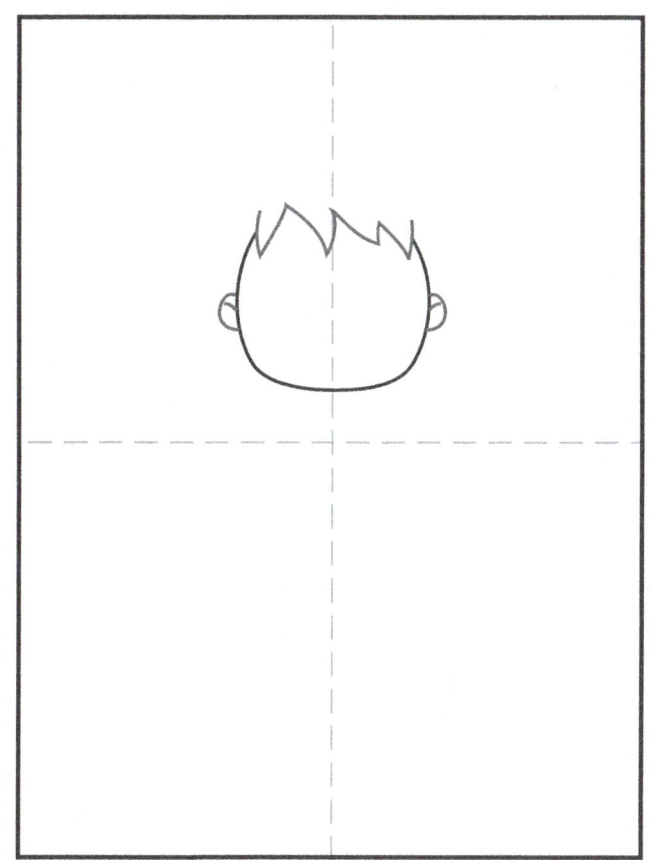

3
Draw the outer hair line.

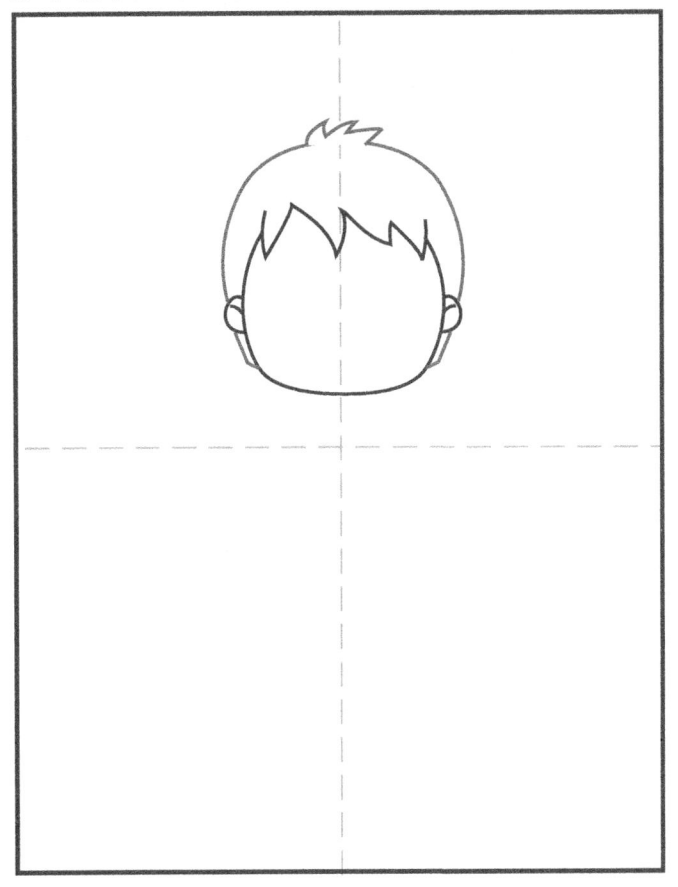

4
Add the face as shown.

5
Draw the scarf and coat.

6
Add the hand, wand, shirt, pants.

7
Draw a simple owl.

8
Add arm, bushes and moon.

Color

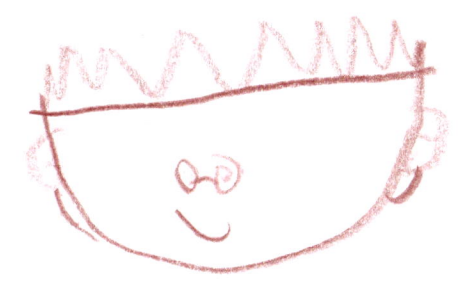

1
Draw the head with bangs.

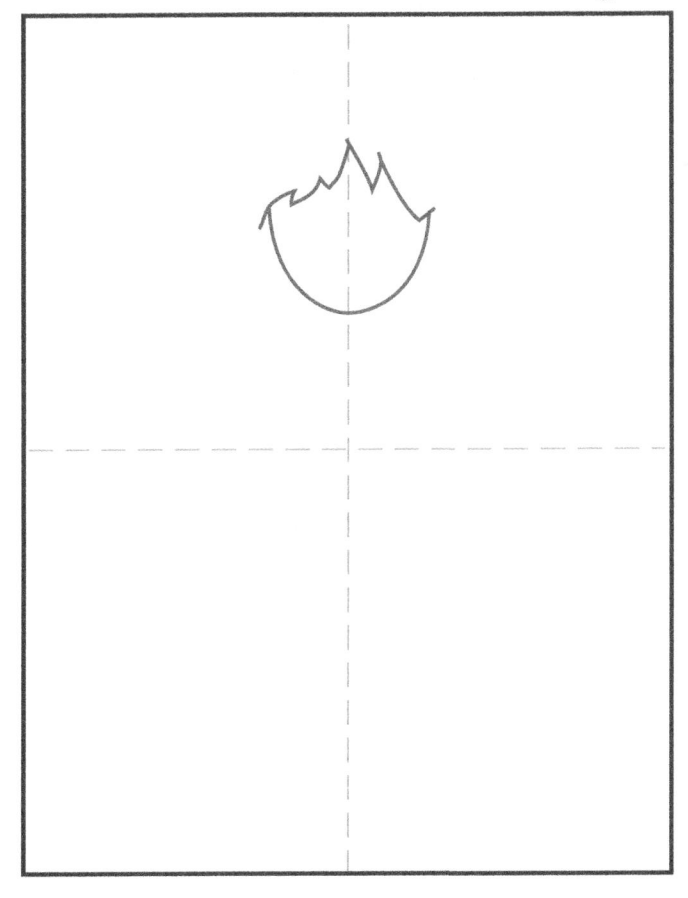

2
Fill in the face. Draw the neckline.

3
Start the jacket with one sleeve.

4
Add a book at an angle.

5
Draw arm on top, and add hands.

6
Draw legs below.

7
Finish with big, wavy hair.

8
Erase lines, draw background.

Color

1
Draw a large U for the head.

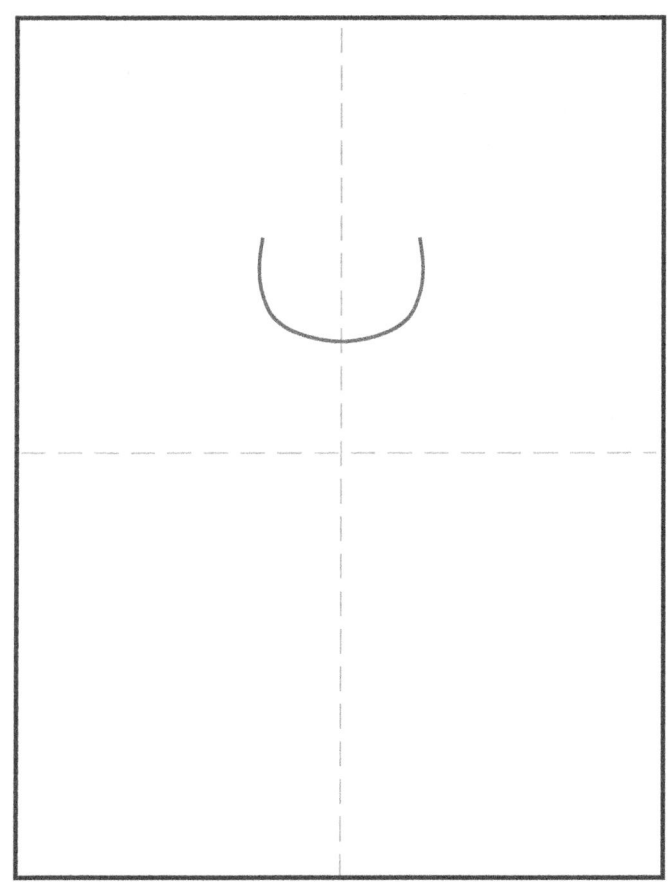

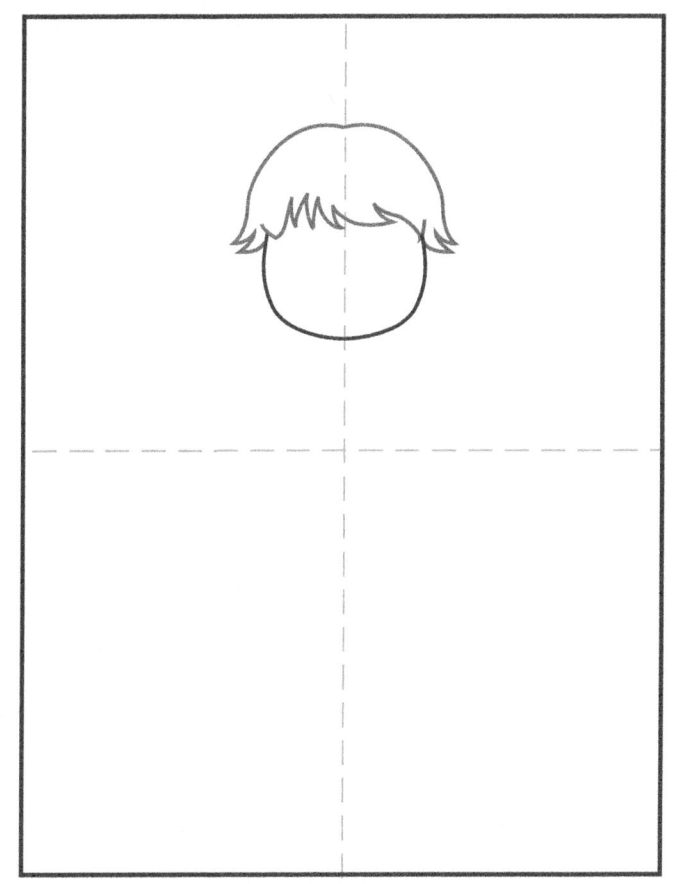

2
Add bushy hair on top

③
Add ears, more hair, and face.

④
Draw the collar and start robe.

5
Finish the robe and neckline.

6
Draw sweater edge, pants, shoes.

7

Add hands, wand, and hills.

8

Draw mountians and buildings.

Color

1
Draw a U shape and hat brim.

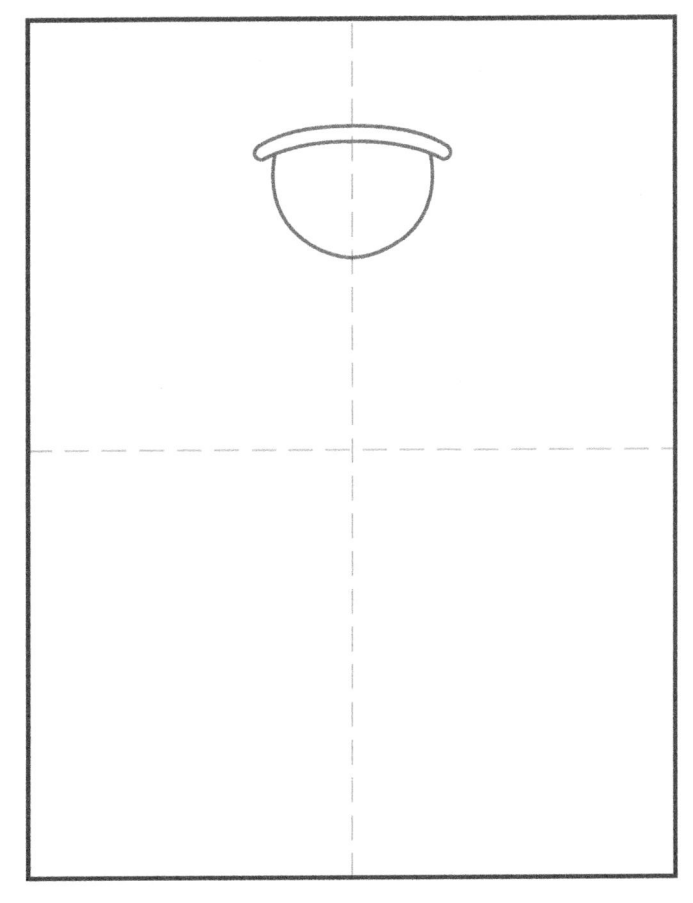

2
Add the hat and beard.

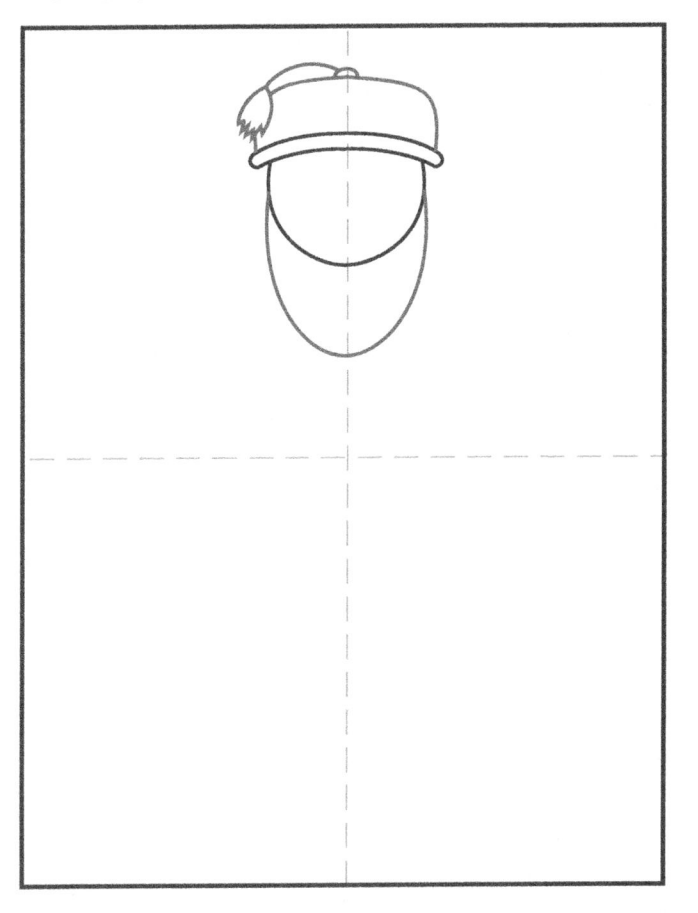

③
Draw the brows and eyes.

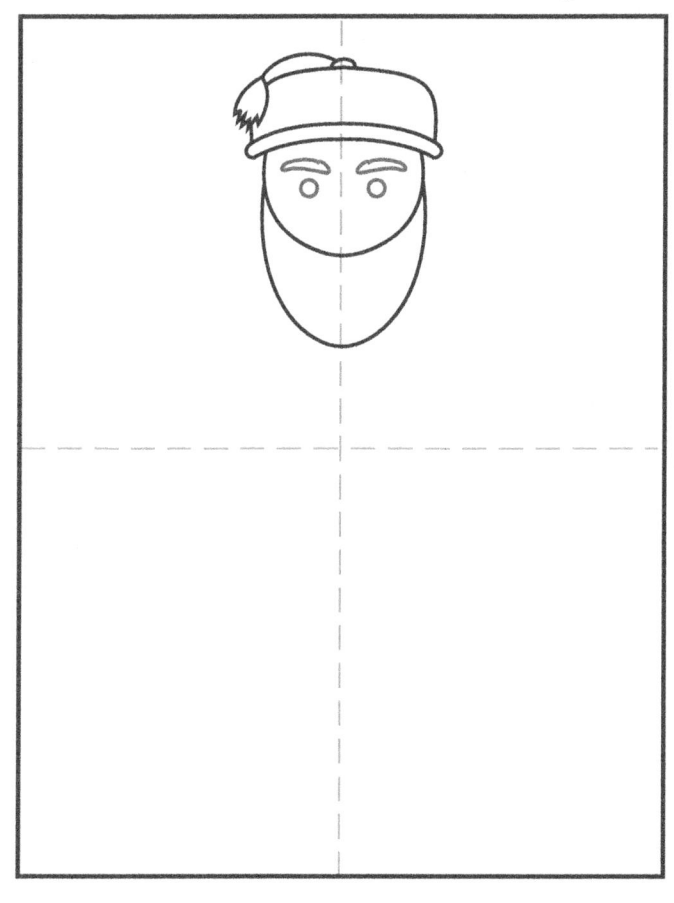

④
Add glasses, nose, moustache.

5
Start the robe, finish beard.

6
Finish the robe and hands.

7
Draw long wavy hair.

8
Add stone texture to background.

Color

Made in the USA
Coppell, TX
25 November 2020